No Money Fun Guidebook...Kaua'i

by Art Jones

To my keiki, the brightest
stars in our night's sky

Maluhia a Aloha

A book by Art Jones, Author 1961-
Cover Design, Book Title, Maps, and Photos are produced,
published, and copyrighted by The Moss Group.

Satellite photography courtesy of NASA
Front cover photo: Kaua'i Chicken
Back cover photo: Kalalau Valley

No Money Fun Guidebook™, registered trademark pending

www.nomoneyfunguidebooks.com

First published in 2012 by
The Moss Group
P.O. Box 1892
Lihue, HI 96766

ISBN# 0-9852718-0-9

Written and published in the U.S.A.
Printed in China

Table of Contents

Introduction..1
Quick Reference...4
Waimea Canyon State Park and Koke'e State Park........5
Touring Hwy. 550...7

Hiking *Makai* Side
Contour Road...8
Kahelu Ridge..9
Papa'alai Road..9
Ha'ele'ele Ridge..9
Polihale Ridge..9
Ka'aweiki Ridge...10
Kauhoa Ridge..10
Makaha Ridge Road...11
Miloli'i Road..12
Nu'alolo Trail..13
Nu'alolo Cliff Trail...14
Awa'awapuhi Trail..16
Honopu Trail...16
Kalepa Trail..18
Pihea Trail..19

Hiking *Mauka* Side
Kukui Trail..20
Waimea Canyon Lookout......................................21
Pu'u Hinahina Lookout...23
Halemanu Road...23
Cliff Trail..24
Canyon Trail..24
Black Pipe Trail...25
Halemanu-Koke'e Trail...25
Faye Trail...26
Mohihi Road..26
Touring Mohihi Road..27
Kumuwela Road...27
Waininiua Trail..27

Kumuwela Trail...28
Puʻu Ka ʻOhelo Trail.....................................28
Berry Flats Trail...28
Ditch Trail..29
Alakaʻi Swamp Trail.......................................30
Alakaʻi Picnic Area...31
Kawaikoi Campground....................................31
Kawaikoi Stream Trail....................................32
Sugi Grove Campground................................33
Waiakoali Campground...................................33
Ditch Road...33
Poʻomau Canyon Vista Trail...........................33
Kohua Ridge Trail..34
Mohihi Trail..35
Water Tank Trail...36
Kaluapuhi Trail...36

Waimea Canyon Base Hikes
Waimea Canyon Trail......................................37
Koaie Canyon Trail...39

South Side Hike
Mahaʻulepu Trail...40

East Side Hikes
Sleeping Giant - Kuamoʻo Nounou Trail...................41
Kuilau Ridge Trail..41
Keahua Arboretum - Loop Road.............................42
Twin Falls / Blue Hole Pools.................................44
Powerline Trail...45
Moalepe Trail...45
Hoʻopiʻi Falls Trail...45

North Shore Hikes
ʻOkolehao Trail..47
Hanakapiʻai Falls Trail.......................................48
Kalalau Trail..50
Kalalau Valley Trail...55

The Kalalau Trail

Beach Combing / Road Tripping

South of Lihu‘e

Kalapaki Beach...57
Menehune Fishpond.......................................57
Tree Tunnel...58
Koloa Town...58
Shipwrecks Beach..59
Po‘ipu Beach Park..60
Koloa Landing...60
Lawa‘i Road and Ho‘ai Beach.............................61
Spouting Horn..62
Kauai Coffee Company.....................................62
Hanapepe Valley Lookout..................................62
Port Allen and Glass Beach................................62
Hanapepe Town..63
Salt Pond Beach Park.......................................63
Russian Fort State Park.....................................64
Waimea Town...64
Waimea Canyon and Koke‘e State Parks.................65
Kikiaola Small Boat Harbor.................................66
Kekaha Beach Park...66
Polihale State Beach..66

North of Lihu'e

'Ahukini Landing.....................................67
Wailua Falls...67
Nukoli'i Beach..68
Lydgate State Beach Park......................68
Wailua Bay..69
Kuamo'o Road.......................................69
Touring Kuamo'o Road..........................70
Old Kapa'a Town....................................70
Kealia Beach...71
Donkey - Kumukumu Beach...................71
Anahola Bay..71
Kong Mountain.......................................72
Moloa'a Bay...72
Larson's Beach......................................72
Rock Quarry - Kahili Beach.....................73
Secret - Kauapea Beach.........................73
Kalihiwai Bay...73
Anini Beach Park....................................74
Hideaway's - Kenomene Beach...............74
Taro Fields Lookout................................74
Hanalei Bay Lookout...............................74
Hanalei Town and Bay.............................75
Kahalahala Beach and Lumahai Beach.....75
Wainiha Bay..76
Tunnels...77
Ha'ena State Beach Park.........................77
Manininiholo Dry Cave.............................77
Waikanaloa and Waikapalae Wet Caves....78
Ke'e Beach..78

Little Money Lots of Fun

Kaua'i Museum...79
Wailua Municipal Golf Course....................79
Limahuli Garden.......................................79
Kilauea Lighthouse and National Wildlife Refuge....80
Kaua'i Mini Golf..81

Glossary

Glossary..82

Waimea Canyon State Park
and
Koke'e State Park

nomoneyfunguidebooks.com

LEGEND

——	Main Highway
——	Paved Roads
- - -	Tote Roads
- ‐ -	Trails
●	Trailheads
△	Campgrounds
●	Lookouts

NA

KALALAU BEACH

NUALOLO LOOKOUT

AWA'AWAPUHI LOOKOUT

HONOP

NU'ALOLO CLIFF TRAIL

AWA'AWAPUHI TR.

NU'ALOLO TRAIL

KOKE'E & LC

MILOLI'I ROAD

KOKE'E STATE PARK

MAKAHA RIDGE ROAD

KAUHOA RIDGE

HALEMANU ROAD

KA'AWEIKI RIDGE

PU'U HINAHINA LOOKOUT

CLIFF TRAIL

POLIHALE STATE BEACH PARK

POLIHALE RIDGE

HA'ELE'ELE RIDGE

CONTOUR ROAD

550

PAPA'ALAI ROAD

KAHELU RIDGE

PAPA'ALAI ROAD

Introduction

Aloha

"No Money Fun Guidebook...Kaua'i" is written to accurately and safely guide you and yours to 55 public hiking trails, lookouts, and *tote roads*; also to 48 adventurous road trips, from beaches to waterfalls, on the beautiful island of Kaua'i. Over the years, your humble author has hiked, swam, drove, and photographed this beloved island.

Kaua'i is a unique place filled with warm-hearted people, pristine valleys, and crystal-clear-blue ocean water. Being the oldest Hawaiian Island at a little over five million years, Kaua'i is a geological infant, yet the Grandmother of Hawai'i, and because of her age she has more sand beach and top soil than any other island. The jungle is thick with a thousand shades of green, the rivers run cool and wide, and the canyons have a beautiful, sienna-colored earth tone which is visually and emotionally striking.

Ocean waters range between 75 and 84 degrees, ambient temperature is about the same during the day. It's always raining somewhere on the island, for dry air go to the west side and for wet, thick jungle to the north shore.

The highways make a giant backwards C around the island, the only part not paved is the magical Na Pali Coast. Your car's odometer and roadside mile marker signs will escort you. Remember to reset your odometer at each turn as this book guides you. All hiking trail distances are measured one way, so don't forget you have to hike back out. Refer to the glossary for Hawaiian, Pidgin, or *italicized* wording.

This is important: drive to "the end of the road" on all of your road trips, there'll be something magnificent waiting for you *mauka* side or *makai*. And please, *no grumble* about spending cash on gas, rentals, or this guidebook to achieve your "No Money Fun" while here at the prettiest spot on Earth…after all, you're on vacation!

Gear

Pack for warm, humid, and wet weather, on a dry day in Kaua'i it will still rain a couple of times. Temperatures year-round range between 70 and 85 degrees during the day with the occasional spike of 95+ degrees on the west side, and as cold as 65 degrees at night on the coastline. Yes, you really have to tough it to live here in the islands. As mentioned, the island tends to be cool and rainy on the north and east coasts, while sunny and drier on the south and west sides. Mountain daytime temperatures (such as at Koke'e State Park) are about 10 degrees cooler, with nights dipping into the 40s or colder at times.

Clothes: waterproof hiking boots, mid-weight with mud tread are important for trail safety, and with good traction you'll burn less energy than slipping around trying to maintain your balance; a waterproof shell pullover, sweatshirt, or fleece; shorts; long pants; t-shirts; and a couple pairs of socks should be enough protection for both day and night.

Drinking water: purifying is necessary, Leptospirosis bacteria is present in stream waters. Water filters, UV light purifiers, or iodine pills all work well to purify. Most prefer using the water purifying pills for the bacteria, they always work, they're lightweight, and aren't prone to mechanical failure. You can also use a coffee filter for the mud, if needed.

There's not always a water source on the trail, so fill up your bottle before the hike, and on day hikes always save more than half of your water for the return hike out to stay hydrated. Kaua'i is very humid and your body will lose water quickly.

Camping needs: food, a three-season tent with an essential rain fly to keep the rain and mosquitos out, a 40+ degree sleeping bag, a camping stove for cooking (camp fires are prohibited at all parks), a flashlight, a collapsable pillow, and a sleeping pad are the basics for camp comfort.

First aid: Band-Aids, a whistle, aspirin or pain reliever of choice. A bandana, hat, mosquito spray (with deet), and sunblock will come in handy.

Beach gear: mask, snorkel and fins, a towel, and bathing suit. Fins help in the strong ocean currents and with a mask you'll feel like you're swimming in a tropical fish tank, great fish colors!

During winter, all Hawaiian Islands have ocean swells from the north with big waves and strong currents. In summer, the swells are from the south. Keep an eye out for county-posted warning signs and swim near lifeguards. Rescue tubes are displayed at beaches island-wide, look for the yellow, orange, or red floaties, and if you need it for rescue, use it. Our water safety slogan is "when in doubt, don't go out", so be safe and enjoy.

Safety

Hiking, swimming, and driving in the Hawaiian Islands have inherent risks, as they do even in your home town. If you feel unsafe at any time, stop what you're doing and return to your comfort zone. "No Money Fun Guidebook™" author and publisher care about your safety. Here are a few safety tips that will help, as the title intends, the Fun continue.

First on my list for safety advice are heavy-treaded hiking boots (for mud) and lots of drinking water (hydration). These are two elements you can control, do so.

While hiking the coastline, be aware of big waves crashing over the rocks. They could knock you off your feet, water is powerful. Wet rocks mean slippery rocks.

Trail conditions are ever-changing. Flash flooding during heavy or continuous rain happens. While crossing streams, keep a good eye upstream. Natural dams can build from fallen trees and when the water pressure is too great, the dam breaks and flash flooding occurs. Hike to high ground and wait until the conditions are safer, be patient.

Quick Reference

Fire and Emergencies: 9-1-1

Police Department: (808) 241-1711

Fire Department: (808) 241-4980

Kaua'i County Lifeguards: (808) 241-4984

Emergency Weather & Traffic Hotline: (808) 241-1725

National Weather Service Lihu'e: (808) 245-6001

Koke'e State Park Weather: (808) 335-9975

Surf Report: (808) 241-7873

State Park Camping Permits: www.hawaiistateparks.org

County Park Camping Permits-

Kapa'a Neighborhood Center: (808) 822-1931

Kalaheo Neighborhood Center: (808) 332-9770

Koke'e Cabin Rentals: www.thelodgeatkokee.net

Kaua'i Bus: www.kauai.gov/visiting or (808) 246-8110

Waimea Canyon State Park and Koke'e State Park

Located on the west side of Kaua'i, Waimea Canyon and Koke'e state parks offer world-class hiking, hunting, and camping. There are two roads to get you to these amazing parks, Hwy. 550 from Waimea town and Hwy. 552 from Kekaha town. The scenic route is Hwy. 550, but both have their own beauty. Hwy. 552 has the ultimate view of sunset over "the Forbidden Island" of Ni'ihau and the atoll of Lehua, about 17 miles off the west coast of Kaua'i, park off the road at MM 6.2, there's space on the soft shoulder.

Hwy. 552 merges with Hwy. 550 as you enter Waimea Canyon State Park, where the curly koa tree jungle starts, look for the 15- to 30-foot shrub-type tree with the light green, sickle (finger-like) leaves.

Licensed vehicles, cars, trucks, dual-sport motorcycles, and mountain bikes are allowed on the *tole roads*, with the latter three recommended; two-wheel drive cars, street bikes, and two-wheel drive trucks have a slippery, fun time on the wet, red clay roads but aren't adequate when the driving gets tough.

Camping, fresh-water fishing, and all hunting are by permit only, they're inexpensive and obtained online at hawaiistateparks.org or visit the third floor of the state building at 3060 'Eiwa St. in Lihu'e. For Koke'e cabin rentals visit www.thelodgeatkokee.net.

While day hiking, pack plenty of water as there's not always a water source on the trail for purifying; an apple; mosquito spray; Band-Aids; a whistle; and a pain reliever of choice. It's always warm and humid in the islands and Koke'e is no exception, however, late afternoon in the hills does get cold, it has even snowed before. So your clothing is important: shorts, t-shirts, a sweatshirt, maybe double socks, and an overcoat for rain and warmth. A heavy-treaded hiking boot or trail sneaker is most important. Again, proper footwear is crucial on Kaua'i, sliding down a 3,000-foot ridge trail is exciting, but dangerous. Also, you'll burn less energy with solid, slip-free footing.

Most people hike trails at an easy, 1 m.p.h. pace to enjoy Mother Nature, super men have rushed the trails at a 2 to 3 m.p.h. pace, time your hikes appropriately and it's always wise to pack a flashlight just in case.

Caution: Contour Road and the six other ridge roads are hunting *tote roads*, hunting is permitted on weekends and holidays, so it's best to avoid these areas, or at least wear a bright-colored bandana or shirt for visibility while hiking all of Waimea and Koke'e, and especially on the hunting *tote roads*.

While sightseeing along Hwy. 550, the first view of the glorious Waimea Canyon is the Kukui Trail at MM 8.7. This life-long memory will only get better as you continue uphill on Hwy. 550 to the lookouts. Don't forget to stop at all the guardrails, these offer a different view of Kaua'i's great canyon.

At MM 12.8 guardrail you'll get the closest full view of Waipo'o Falls, an 800-foot beauty! Remember, summers are dry, it might rain only five times a day. In midwinter, heavy rains mean big waterfalls and colorful rainbows! Winter Koke'e temperatures range from 35 degrees at the coldest of night to 75 degrees midday, summer temperatures range from 50 degrees at nighttime to 80 degrees at high noon in the parks. MM 13.7 will bring you to Pu'u HinaHina Lookout, the furthest north lookout the canyon has to offer.

At MM 14.1, Koke'e State Park begins and

continues to "the end of the road". At MM 15.4 is the Koke'e Natural History Museum, Koke'e Lodge Restaurant (also the check-in location for cabin rentals), and the only campground with flush toilets and showers.

Behind the museum is a short 0.2 mile nature trail, a recommended appetizer to Koke'e's superlative trails, with numbered plaques to identify the trees and shrubs, reference cards are available at the museum.

MM 18 is the Kalalau Valley Lookout, an impressive side view of this famous green valley with crisp, clean air, huge altitudes, cloud-level skies, and clear-blue ocean. Picnic tables and last-chance flush toilets are on site.

At MM 20, the end of the road, is Pu'u O Kila Lookout, "the Prettiest Spot on Earth"...for real, but I'll let you gather your own impressions! In winter get here, as well as MM 18, in

TOURING HWY. 550

8.7 MM Kukui Trail *p.20*

10.4MM Waimea Canyon Lookout *p.21*

11.1MM Contour Rd. *p.8*

13.2MM Kauhoa Ridge *p.10*

13.7MM Pu'u HinaHina Lookout *p.22*

13.9MM Makaha Rd. *p.11*

- Miloli'i Rd. *p.12*

14.1MM Hulemanu Rd. *p.22*

- Canyon Trail *p.23*
- Cliff Trail *p.23*
- Black Pipe Trail *p.24*
- Halemanu-Koke'e Trail *p.24*

4.1/15.1MM No Name Rd.

15.3MM Nu'alolo Trail *p.13*

- Nu'alolo Cliff Trail *p.14*

15.4MM Koke'e Lodge & Museum

15.5 MM Mohihi Rd. *p.25*

- Waininiua Trail *p.26*
- Kumuwela Trail *p.27*
- Pu'u Ka 'Ohelo Trail *p.27*
- Berry Flats Trail *p.27*
- Ditch Trail *p.28*
- Alaka'i Swamp Trail *p.29*
- Kawaikoi Stream Trail *p.31*
- Po'omau Canyon Vista
- Mohihi Trail *p.34*

15.9MM Water Tank Trail *p.35*

17.1MM Awa'awapuhi Trail *p.15*

17.3MM Kaluapuhi Trail *p.35*

17.5MM Honopu Trail *p.17*

18MM Kalalau Lookout

- Kalepa Trail *p.17*

20MM Pu'u O Kila Lookout

- Pihea Trail *p.18*

the morning before the afternoon clouds roll in, it does white out, but it will pass and it's well worth the wait. Pu'u O Kila is a favorite drive-to site, top of the list, it's also the Pihea trailhead. Hike down the wide, slippery trail to get your best full valley views. This earthly view will reward, rejoice, and rejuvenate any wary soul. I've always felt a warm comfort here...even on a cool day. It's a must-see, enjoy! Waimea Canyon State Park is 1,866.4 acres and Koke'e State Park is 4,345 acres.

Hiking *Makai* Side
Contour Road

Moderate effort
6.2 miles
Elevation gain 30 feet

Hwy. 550, MM 11.1. Turn at the Papa'alai trailhead sign. Drive 1.2 miles to the start of Contour Road, this is the trailhead to Papa'alai Trail and a stone's throw from Kahelu Trail.

Contour Road is a 6.2-mile, four-wheel drive, switchback, *tote road* that parallels the highway. It's an alluring and easy drive or it makes for great, claustrophobic-free hiking. Jungle lines the road of this seldom-used portion of Waimea Canyon.

This road brings you to hunting trails 1 through 6. Trails 1 and 2 are hunting *tote roads* in the Kekaha Game Management Area, off limits to hikers. Trail 3 offers a birds-eye-view of Kekaha, and trails 4 through 6 will bring you to the amazing cliffs of the Na Pali Coast. There are yellow gates at each trailhead, if open, you can drive, if not, then hike.

Kahelu Ridge

Moderate effort
4.6 miles
Elevation gain 472 feet
Contour Road, Mile 0, hunting trail 1. This is a hunting trail only, off limits to hiking. A silty, fine-dirt *tote road* that brings you through the Kekaha Game Management Area. The better Na Pali views are hunting trails 3 through 6, with trail 6 as the ultimate.

Papaʻalal Road

Moderate effort
5.4 miles and forks to 7.6 or 8.8 miles
Elevation gain 620 feet
Contour Road, Mile 0, hunting trail 2. This is a hunting trail only, off limits to hiking. A *tote road* that is also part of the Kekaha Game Management Area.

Haʻeleʻele Ridge

Moderate effort
3.3 miles
Elevation gain 1,578 feet
Contour Road, MM 2.3, hunting trail 3. The jungle starts to thicken at this point, and at the end of the trail there's a view looking straight down onto Polihale State Beach.

   The road has a short hunting trail to the left at about the halfway point, and further down the *tote road* you'll reach a fork to the right that's 1.3 miles and will get you a bit closer to the overlook of Polihale State Beach.

Polihale Ridge

Moderate effort
3.1 miles
Elevation gain 1,611 feet

Contour Road, MM 3.8, hunting trail 4. A 3.1 mile road that has a small fork at the end. This is your first good view of the Na Pali Coast and her bold charm.

Lush jungle begins with this *tote road* and continues to thicken on the hiking trails further north (see the following ridge trails). This is a good starting point if you're going to hike the Contour Road area, and it's also 4x4 drivable.

Ka'aweiki Ridge

Moderate effort
3.5 miles
Elevation gain 1,549 feet
Contour Road, MM 5.2, hunting trail 5. A 3.5 mile *tote road* that offers the first birds-eye-view looking straight down onto blue, blue ocean, with Hikimoe Valley to the south and Ka'aweiki Valley to the north.

Kauhoa Ridge

Moderate effort
3.4 miles
Elevation gain 1,552 feet
Contour Road, MM 6, hunting trail 6. A 3.4 mile *tote road* that's a bit steeper than the other ridge roads.

From this trail you'll get outstanding southern views of two ridges in the foreground, the brilliance of Polihale State Beach, the island of Ni'ihau, and the atoll of Lehua. There are a few pools of the soft, silty dirt on this road, dual-sport and mountain bikers beware! If you are going to hike only one hunting trail *tote road*, Kauhoa is recommended.

Contour Road

Congratulations! This is the end of Contour Road, a great hiking, 4x4, dual-sport motorcycle, and mountain bike fun zone. To get back to Hwy. 550 drive straight out on Kauhoa *tote road* for 1 mile, passing Contour Road and cottages, then you'll arrive back on the highway at MM 13.2.

Makaha Point

Makaha Ridge Road

High effort
4.1 miles
Elevation gain 1,900 feet

Hwy. 550, MM 13.9. A paved road that leads to Miloli'i Ridge *tote road*, Makaha Ridge trailhead, and a U.S. Navy post at the end.

At 0.3 miles on the right is the Miloli'i trailhead, a 5.1 mile *tote road* that's 4x4 drivable to the top of the cliffs on Na Pali's coastline. Breathtaking views of Miloli'i Valley, Keawanui Point, sand beach to the north, a lava rock beach to the south, and the magnificent, shallow, jade-colored ocean are all from these excitingly-high elevations.

At 3.4 miles on the left is the Makaha Ridge trailhead, a 4x4 (expert drivers only) *tote road*. Look for tire tracks, if they end, then you should park and hike to your destination, the locals know the jungle *tote roads*. 1.3 miles will take you to the point, a rolling red dirt wonder, think Mars! At 3.8 miles, there's a nice drive-to view of Miloli'i Valley, simply climb the 10-foot red dirt mound on the right.

Miloli'i Point

Miloli'i Road

Moderate effort
5.1 miles
Elevation gain 1,827 feet
Hwy. 550, MM 13.9. Turn onto Makaha Ridge Road, drive 0.3 miles to the gated Miloli'i trailhead.

A maintained *tote road* with a few mud holes in the first mile and soft silt towards the point. This is four-wheel drivable all the way to the Na Pali Coast rim. On a dry day, it's possible (at your own risk) to drive your two-wheel drive family car to the picnic table area at MM 2.5. Park and hike the wide, pine tree-lined *tote road* to the majestic Miloli'i Ridge point. Many will love this ridge with its high views of Miloli'i Valley to the north and birds-eye-view of Keawanui Point.

Just a 15-minute hike from your parking spot up the ridge to the point and you'll get the grand prize, a mesmerizing view of the warm Pacific Ocean. Off-shore rains bring intense rainbows, remember to use your polarizer filter while photographing to capture the saturated rainbow colors!

Nu'alolo Trail

High effort
3.8 miles
Elevation gain 2,034 feet
Hwy. 550, MM 15.3. Roadside parking for about 10 cars at the trailhead but it's best to park at the museum's large parking lot and hike downhill 0.1 mile.

A single-track trail that starts with a short, uphill climb, then mostly all downhill (as with all the *makai* trails) to the Na Pali Coast and her outstanding views to the north. The first portion of the trail is a wide, spacious valley hike with moderate elevation drops. You'll enjoy lots of jungle canopy, strawberry guava, and red Awa'awapuhi ginger. It's the muddy part of the trail, even on a dry day, with slippery tree roots underfoot, use your walking stick.

The first fork is just after the halfway mark, this is a shortcut to a picnic table that is close to the south end of Nu'alolo Cliff trailhead. The actual Nu'alolo Cliff trailhead is another mile or so west of this shortcut and 0.5 miles before the trail's end, stay on the main trail to reach the jaw- dropping Nuʻalolo Lookout.

The second portion of Nuʻalolo Trail is open air with little shade and great views, the trail narrows into erosion troughs in places with steeper elevation drops until you reach the lookout point. From the lookout, there's the impressive vertical-walled Nuʻalolo Valley, huge northern Na Pali coastline views starting with Nuʻalolo Beach, Kalalau Beach, then Keʻe Beach and endless clear, blue ocean. This place is special and will reward you by easing the pains of being human, it is breathtaking.

Hiking sticks are a wonderful safety tool and they also reduce leg and back fatigue. Pack all the water you and yours will need, remember to save more than half of your water for the trek out, your body will be working a lot harder climbing back out to the highway. It will take about 6 hours round trip at a leisurely pace; you know, photos, lunch, mate pleasuring, and the like.

Nuʻalolo Trail also loops with Nuʻalolo Cliff Trail and Awaʻawapuhi Trail for a total of 11.4 miles, this includes back tracking from both lookouts 0.8 miles, and 1.7 miles on the highway to get back to your car. The loop is an ambitious and gratifying full-circle hike, it's legendary! Most like to hike the loop from the south to north only for the downhill finale on the highway hike back to the car. The loop is about an 9-hour hike at an easy pace.

Nuʻalolo Cliff Trail
High effort
2 miles
Elevation gain 381 feet
A high effort only because you need to hike Awaʻawapuhi

Trail or Nuʻalolo Trail for about 3 miles to hook up with Nuʻalolo Cliff Trail.

A tight, single-track trail with beautiful views from the back of the valley cliffs and links to two beautiful lookout points on Na Pali. Don't count on a water source on this trail or while hiking the entire loop, there are streams crossing Nuʻalolo Cliff Trail but they do run dry. At 0.3 miles south of Awaʻawapuhi Trail look for a 25-foot waterfall during the rainy season. During the fall months there's a lot of strawberry guava, a gumball-sized red fruit, look for the dark maroon ones and mind the seeds.

Awaʻawapuhi Lookout

Awaʻawapuhi Trail

High effort
3.1 miles
Elevation gain 1,847 feet

Hwy. 550, MM 17.1. Plenty of field parking at the trailhead. A wide, single-track trail that's all downhill to the lookout point. It's all canopied jungle for shade with lots of botany and bird watching. Look for pig and goat on your early morning or late afternoon treks. A well-maintained trail by the Kokeʻe State Park *hui*, it's a popular trail with lots of foot traffic for the social hiker.

The point offers breathtaking, steep views of Awaʻawapuhi Valley and Honopu Ridge to the west, then Nuʻalolo Valley and the Pacific's crystal-clear ocean to the south. As always, save more than half of your water for the climb out to your car, it's all uphill. A 6-hour round-trip hike at an easy pace. These valleys are spectacular, enjoy.

Honopu Trail

High effort
Approximately 3.5 miles
Elevation gain 1,512 feet

Hwy. 550, MM 17.5. An unmaintained trail. Long pants and sleeves will protect your skin against dry fern scrapes on this narrow, single-track trail. Colored ribbons mark the Honopu Trail and other lessor hiked trails on the island. Hunting and pig trails fork off the main trail, it's important to follow the heavily-traveled path.

About halfway you'll be ducking under and hopping over trees, *small kine*. The final push to the point is steep with plenty loose dirt and overhangs. Thinking about safety, heavy-treaded boots will help with traction along with a hiking stick.

At the point, the trail swings south for more views of Na Pali rim real estate than any other of Koke'e's *makai* trails. Spectacular views of the old taro fields, lava rock spires, and miles of elevated coastline will refresh your mind and soul. An adventurous 6-hour hike and I know you'll *talk story*...forever, enjoy!

Honopu View

Kalepa Trail

Kalepa Trail

Moderate Effort
Approximately 1.5 miles
Elevation gain 1,585 feet

Hwy. 550, MM 18. Park at the Kalalau Valley Lookout lot. Almost every step of Kalepa Ridge offers unobstructed views of the mighty Kalalau Valley.

The trailhead is to the left of the viewing rail. You will be hiking on the valley's edge for the most part, watch your feet while hiking and stop completely when looking around, drinking water, or shooting photos. Safety first! The beginning is a narrow, single-track trail that descends through scratchy, dried fern branches for a few hundred feet, long pants or leg gators will help you retain at least a pint of blood.

You'll be hiking along the rim starting halfway down the trail until the point with excitingly-fun, elevated views of the valley's floor to the ocean. While standing on Kalepa Trail, you can look straight past your toes down 3,000 feet into the valley! If you have difficulty with height anxieties, step back and acclimate for a few minutes, you'll adjust and be fine. There's a wonderful perch a hundred yards from the point, overlooking Kalalau Beach and the valley's magnificent spires. A memorable, 3-hour hike.

Pihea Trail

Moderate effort
4.7 miles
Elevation gain 719 feet

The end of Hwy. 550, MM 20. Park and walk up the paved hill to the trailhead and Pu'u O Kila Lookout.

For a great day hike, hike straight ahead 1 mile to the Pihea Lookout, the highest elevation in Koke'e State Park at 4,283 feet At 0.8 miles, the trail continues *mauka* to complete the 3.7 mile Pihea Trail. This trail ends at the Kawalkol Campground on Mohihi Road, 7 miles away from the Pu'u O Kila Lookout, so it's shorter to back-track on Pihea Trail to reach your car.

The first 0.75 miles is a wide and slippery path that overlooks the prettiest spot on Earth, the Kalalau Valley, and here you'll be centered on the rim for the ultimate, elevated, 4,000-foot views. One of the largest valleys in the state of Hawai'i, with her thousand shades of green and the bluest ocean water ever seen. Fern and 'Ohi'a trees (in full bloom late summer to fall) line the trail, with plenty bird watching.

The trail turns off on the *mauka* side to continue the Pihea Trail, or hike straight ahead and climb the three 40 -foot root and rock-embedded walls to get to the Pihea Lookout. Back at the *mauka* fork, you'll hike downhill on wooden steps to a boardwalk crossing the Alaka'i Swamp Trail, then the trail switchbacks down a single-track to the Kawaikoi Stream and campground.

Please hike on the boardwalk, there are tons of rare plants all around. Respect them, they might be the cure. A 5-hour hike at an easy pace.

This completes the *makai* side of Waimea Canyon State Park and Koke'e State Park and I know your Na Pali Coast memories will last you a lifetime. Now go and boat the ocean to get the total Na Pali Coast viewing experience!

Hiking *Mauka* Side
Kukui Trail

High Effort
2.5 miles
Elevation gain about 2,240 feet
Hwy. 550, MM 8.7. Roadside parking. This is the only roadside trail from the canyon's rim on Hwy. 550 that brings you to the floor of the Waimea Canyon. This steep trail starts to the right on the Iliau Nature Loop by the picnic table, then it's a switchback, single-track trail for about a mile.

At 1.2 miles the Kukui Trail turns left at a directional sign, or for a 3-hour half-day hike go straight up the hill for a high-cliff, perched view of the Waimea River (a stream at this point) and great canyon views. Continuing down trail to the Waimea River, you'll descend a wide, red dirt wash and then into a single-track jungle trail to the Wiliwili Campsite and the river, where the Kukui Trail ends.

From Wiliwili Camp, head left on the Waimea Canyon Trail (a *tote road*) to Kaluahaulu Campground, about a quarter mile north of Wiliwili. Kaluahaulu Camp is recommended for it's pristine swimming holes and serenity. From here, the Koaie Trail starts and continues for 3 miles, passing Hipalau Camp and ending at Lonomea Campsite. Koaie Canyon is one of the most spectacular canyons in the world, its steep walls keep it well-guarded. Also, to camp overnight with the goat, pig, and black-tailed deer is pretty cool.

Okay, back to Kukui Trail, pack more water than you think you'll need, at least 1.5 liters, with a water source at the river to purify for further hydration. Hiking this trail is all descent, then ascent. As a day hike, it is doable but at a super man effort, a 5-hour hike.

Waimea Lookout

Waimea Canyon Lookout

Hwy. 550, MM 10.4. A drive-to lookout with lots of parking, flush toilets, and a snack vendor. The magnificent Waimea Canyon will amaze. A short hike uphill (there's also a wheelchair accessible ramp) will bring you to two viewing platforms, the lower of these offers an up close and personal Waimea Canyon experience. At 14 miles long, 1 mile wide, and 3,600 feet deep, this exceptional canyon will leave aghast all those fortunate to gaze upon her unique beauty.

The views from the safety fence platforms are the Koaie Canyon (straight ahead at your 12 o'clock), Po'omau Canyon (at 11 o'clock), and Waipo'o Falls (10 o'clock), an 800-foot waterfall that flows in the rainy winter months or on soggy summer days. Take your time, hours or days, to enjoy Mother Nature's sublimity. Kaua'i's Waimea Canyon is a spectacle whose memories will last forever.

At MM 12.8 on Hwy. 550, there's a short guardrail that offers the closest full view of Waipo'o Falls, a great photo opportunity. Stopping at all the guardrails on will give you a fresh perspective of this magnificent canyon, enjoy!

Waimea Canyon Arches

Pu'u HinaHina Lookout

Hwy. 550, MM 13.7. A drive-to lookout with lots of parking and flush toilets. A short, 100-foot walk will get you to a viewing platform. This is the location for a view of the entire north side of the canyon, from the Wai'ahulu Stream, all the way down the canyon, to the Pacific Ocean. There's also a short trail to the left of the restrooms which overlooks "the Forbidden Island" of Ni'ihau and atoll of Lehua. Sunrise visits are sensational and goats are plentiful.

At the back of the parking lot is an unmarked, single-track trail that switchbacks through old growth koa trees and wonderful, pristine jungle, then joins with Canyon Trail, Black Pipe Trail, and Cliff viewpoint (a lookout). This location completes the west rim of the Waimea Canyon that are off of Hwy. 550 and reachable by family car

Halemanu Road

Hwy. 550, MM 14.1. This is the start of Koke'e State Park. A 1.2 mile *tote road* leading to five trailheads. You can park off Hwy. 550 and hike, or it's four-wheel drivable.

The first fork to the right at MM 0.6 takes you to the Cliff Trail Lookout and the trailhead for Canyon Trail, at 0.8 miles is the Black Pipe trailhead, and at 1 mile you'll pick up the south end of Halemanu-Koke'e Trail. There are year-round residents who live in the cabins in this part of Koke'e (luckies), so please park considerately and always pack out your trash.

Cliff Trail

Easy effort
0.6 miles
Elevation gain less than 100 feet
Hwy. 550, MM 14.1-Halemanu *tote road*. Drive (4x4) or hike 0.6 miles and turn right at first fork, drive 0.1 miles to parking and the trailhead.

A short trail that leads to a safety-railed clearing. An excellent view of Waimea Canyon's steep and narrow northwest walls.

Canyon Trail

High effort
1.8 miles
Elevation gain 246 feet
Hwy. 550, MM 14.1-Halemanu *tote road*. Drive (4x4) or hike 0.6 miles, then turn right at the first fork and go 0.1 miles to parking at the trailhead. A favorite among the canyon trails, it has jungle, water, and huge canyon views.

A single-track, switchback trail that hikes through a valley of koa trees to a red dirt bald spot for your first canyon view. At the far side of the baldy vista look south to the adjacent rim, across Koke'e Stream, for great views of the lava arches. Hike down into the valley and you're at Waipo'o Falls, follow the path *mauka* through the white ginger fields (in bloom mid to late summer) a couple hundred feet to baby Waipo'o Falls, a 25-footer with a swimming hole, enjoy the cool down and look for ancient petroglyphs carved into the lava rock, they're around!

Cross the stream and continue uphill to the next red dirt bald spot, this is the greatest Waimea Canyon lookout Kaua'i has to offer and there's a picnic table. To the east is Po'omau Canyon and at your 11 o'clock is Kohua Ridge, also an excellent hiking trail. Please pack superglue with your gear, you'll need it to glue your eyes back in your head, it's that glorious! *Aloha* and *mahalo Pele*.

Hiking east will get you back into the jungle with a single-track, switchback trail for about 0.7 miles to exit at Kumuwela viewpoint and *tote road*. A 4-hour hike at a slow pace with a swim and photos. Elevation gain of 246 feet at start and finish points but remember you'll hike three valleys on this trail.

Black Pipe Trail

Moderate effort
0.5 miles
Elevation gain 322
Hwy. 550, MM 14.1-Halemanu Road. Drive or hike 0.8 miles to the trailhead sign and park. The *tote road* continues 0.2 miles and at the first fork go right.

A single-track trail that switchbacks down through a koa tree jungle. About halfway into the valley the trail forks again, go right and hike the valley's rim with great canyon views until it joins with the Canyon Trail.

Halemanu-Koke'e Trail

Easy effort
1.2 miles
Elevation gain less than 250 feet
Hwy. 550, MM 14.1-Halemanu Road. Drive (4x4) or hike 1 mile to Halemanu-Koke'e trailhead. A wide, single-track trail that hikes up and over a hill. Lots of koa trees, old-growth jungle, and fields of Portuguese Lilies (in full

bloom mid to late summer), it's a beautiful trail.

Faye Trail

A short trail, 0.1 miles, at the end of Halemanu *tote road* that basically links local cabin duelers, a neighborhood thing. Want to make a new friend in Hawai'i? Bring the *braughda* a fish.

No Name Road

Hwy. 550, MM 14.4 to MM 15.1. A short *tote road* shaped like a boomerang that leads to Koke'e cabins, no need bother the *braughdas*.

Mohihi Road

Moderate effort
6.2 miles
Elevation gain 280 feet
Hwy. 550, MM 15.5. Look for the Camp Sloggett sign to start this 6.2-mile, four-wheel drive *tote road* that leads to some of the best *mauka* hiking in Koke'e. Twelve trails in all, a handful of other *tote roads*, five covered picnic table areas, Kawaikoi, Sugi Grove, Waiakoali, and Koaie campgrounds.

At 0.9 miles, take the fork to the right (a tricky spot) to continue, left goes to Pu'u Ka 'Ohelo Trail and the rental cabins a quarter mile in.

The road is maintained and drivable, and at your own risk you can drive your two-wheel drive family car 1.6 miles to the last-chance parking space, then hike or 4x4 the rest of the road.

Kumuwela Road

Hwy. 550, MM 15.5 — see Touring Mohihi Road. Drive or hike 1.3 miles down Mohihi *tote road* to the beginning of Kumuwela *tote road*.

A 2-mile, four-wheel drive *tote road* that brings you to Waininiua Trail, Kumuwela Trail, and the east end of Canyon Trail (a great way to enjoy Canyon Trail).

Waininiua Trail

Easy effort
0.6 miles
Hwy. 550, MM 15.5 — see Touring Mohihi Road. Drive or hike 1.3 miles to Kumuwela *tote road*, then 0.4 miles to the Waininiua trailhead.

A tight, single-track trail with lots of strawberry guava in October and November. There's a short erosion trough on the downhill side to be navigated, *small kine*. Good birding and pristine jungle awaits.

For a wonderful 2-hour jungle loop, start at Waininiua trailhead, hike to the neighboring *tote road,* and head south less than a quarter mile to the Kumuwela trailhead. Hike the valley and good-sized hill that ends

---

TOURING MOHIHI ROAD

0.9MM FORK
- right to continue Mohihi Rd.
- left to Pu'u Ka 'Ohelo Trail *p.27*

1.3MM Kumuwela Rd *p.26*
- Waininiua Trail *p.26*
- Kumuwela Trail *p.27*

1.4MM Berry Flats Trail *p.27*

1.7MM Ditch Trail *p.28*

3MM FORK
- left to Alaka'i Swamp Trail *p.29*
- middle to continue Mohihi Rd.
- right to Alaka'i Picnic Area *p.30*

3.6MM Kawaikoi Camp *p.30*

3.7MM Kawaikoi Trail *p.31*
- Sugi Grove Camp *p.31*

4.2MM Walakoali Camp *p.31*

4.5MM FORK
- left to continue Mohihi Rd.
- right to Ditch Rd. *p.32*

4.6MM Po'omau Canyon Vista Trail *p.32*

5.2MM Kohua Ridge Trail *p.33*

6.2MM End of the road
- Mohihi Trail *p.34*
- Koaie Campground

---

at the Kumuwela *tote road* and go northeast back to Waininiua trailhead.

Kumuwela Trail

Moderate effort
1 mile

Hwy. 550, MM 15.5—see Touring Mohihi Road. Drive or hike 1.3 miles to Kumuwela *tote road*, then 1.7 miles to the Kumuwela trailhead.

A wonderful, single-track jungle trail that hikes up and over one of the highest viewing points *mauka* side in Koke'e. Lots of birds, fields of ginger, and a couple of small clearings make for diverse scenery.

Pu'u Ka 'Ohelo Trail

Easy effort
0.4 miles
Elevation gain less than 100 feet

Hwy. 550, MM 15.5—see Touring Mohihi Road. Drive or hike 0.9 miles to the fork, go left, then continue 0.2 miles to the trailhead.

A short, jungle trail with lots of old-growth eucalyptus, guava trees, and moss-covered jungle. It joins the Water Tank Trail to the left and will take you close to the Koke'e Museum, going right will loop you onto Berry Flats Trail.

Berry Flats Trail

Easy effort
0.6 miles
Elevation gain flat

Hwy. 550, MM 15.5—see Touring Mohihi Road. Drive or hike 1.4 miles to the trailhead. There's a small parking spot across the road.

This is the flattest trail on Kaua'i. Redwood forest and fields of moss-covered goodies make for outstanding photography. The redwood trees have a shallow root mass and with the island's strong winds there are lots of toppled trees with 20-foot root structures pointing towards the sky. The wide forest space is also unique for this island, compared to the thick jungle. Cub Scouts take advantage by building stick-and-thatch roof lean-tos. Their village looks like days gone by, an easier time.

Ditch Trail

Moderate effort
1.7 miles

Hwy. 550, MM 15.5—see Touring Mohihi Road. Drive or hike 2.3 miles to the trailhead. Remember, you can drive your two-wheel drive car to the 1.6-mile last-chance parking and hike the 0.7 miles downhill to the trailhead, or there's a small 4x4 parking field just 0.1 mile past the trailhead.

A tight, single-track trail that follows the north rim of Po'omau Canyon. First, you'll descend and cross the stream where you'll see a cool, hand-carved irrigation ditch tunnel, then climb up a short distance to the rim with beautiful, green valley views.

About 25 minutes in there's a fork, a gift to you is to go left, this takes you onto a short ridge with the only birds-eye-view of Moeloa Falls, a three-tiered 400-foot beauty, and the respectfully smaller Kawaikoi Falls to the left. There's an excellent view straight ahead of Po'omau Canyon Lookout.

The Ditch Trail ends at a *tote road* for a 3-mile hike back to your car, so it's recommended to hike the Ditch

Trail back, it's the shorter distance.

There's Poʻomau Stream access downhill 0.1 mile on Mohihi Road from the Ditch trailhead, look for a small grass parking spot (4x4 accessible only) and follow the trail. Ice cold winter waters offer quick and stimulating cool downs.

Kīlohana Lookout

Alakaʻi Swamp Trail

Moderate effort
3.5 miles
Elevation gain 213 feet

Hwy. 550, MM 15.5—see Touring Mohihi Road. Drive (4x4 only) or hike 3 miles to a location sign, take a left and go 0.3 miles to the trailhead.

Most of this trail is a boardwalk with a clanky, metal mesh on top for traction (loud but needed). Bird watchers be patient and still, they will fly back when all is quiet. Please stay on the boardwalk, there's a lot of endangered plant life in Alakaʻi Swamp!

The trail crosses the Pihea Trail, then continues forward to hike two valleys. The first being the larger with a cool stream at the base, a good water source but please sterilize your drinking water, Leptospirosis bacteria is present.

After the valleys, the boardwalk begins again all the way to the magnificent Kilohana Lookout overlooking Hanalei Bay and the pristine Wainiha Valley. The swamp itself is a primordial ooze, bubbling and mystical with palettes full of earth-tone colors to delight. It's also the highest elevated swamp in the world at 4,000 feet. A 5-hour hike at a slow pace. Elevation gain of 213 deceptive feet...remember the two valleys to hike.

Alaka'i Picnic Area

Hwy. 550, MM 15.5—see Touring Mohihi Road. Drive (4x4 only) or hike 3 miles to the picnic area on the right. Wonderful views of Po'omau Canyon and Kohua Ridge, with covered tables, and an outhouse. Life is good!

Kawaikoi Campground

Hwy. 550, MM 15.5—see Touring Mohihi Road. Drive (4x4 only) or hike 3.6 miles to the beautifully groomed Kawaikoi Campground, a mowed half-acre field with a covered picnic table and outhouse. It's an open field, so canopy shade is...not.

It's the south end of Pihea Trail with Kawaikoi Stream, Sugi Grove Campground, and Kawaikoi Stream Trail all a stone's throw away. Camping by permit only.

Kawaikoi Stream Trail

Kawaikoi Stream Trail

Easy effort
1.8 miles
Elevation gain 40 feet

Hwy. 550, MM 15.5—see Touring Mohihi Road. Drive (4x4 only) or hike 3.7 miles to the Kawaikoi Stream trailhead on the left, across from Sugi Grove Campground. The Kawaikoi Stream crosses Mohihi Road, if you're concerned about the water's depth, carefully walk it on-foot first before crossing in your truck.

A single-track trail, well-maintained, that starts in the old-growth Sugi Pine forest with toppled, moss-covered trees. You then hike the loop along the stream and back to the trailhead. Water people will love this trail, one of the few stream-side trails on Kaua'i, it's lush with plenty of wildlife.

There are two stream crossings as the trail loops back to Mohihi Road, which requires a little rock-hopping action. The dry rocks aren't as slippery as wet ones. Fields of yellow ginger and strawberry guava (in season September through November) line this poetic trail.

Sugi Grove Campground

Hwy. 550, MM 15.5—see Touring Mohihi Road. Drive (4x4 only) or hike 3.7 miles to Sugi Grove Campground.

There's a tall, old-growth Sugi Pine grove that offers lots of shade, an outhouse, and the lower Kawaikoi Stream with it's huge boulders to play on. Permit camping only.

Waiakoali Campground

Hwy. 550, MM 15.5—see Touring Mohihi Road. Drive (4x4 only) or hike 4.2 miles to a nice and secluded picnic area. You'll find a covered picnic table, mowed grass, jungle views, an outhouse, and plenty privacy. Camping by permit.

Ditch Road

Hwy. 550, MM 15.5—see Touring Mohihi Road. Drive (4x4 only) or hike 4.5 miles. This *tote road* parallels Mohihi Road for 2.4 miles to a picnic area.

It's a tight, almost not drivable, 4x4 road with 3-foot deep mud holes. Therefore, it's good to park at the beginning (roadside) for a 0.3 mile walk to Po'omau Canyon Lookout Trail, it also crosses Kohua Trail, and then Mohihi Trail at the end of the road. However, it's best to park and hike from the Mohihi Road trailheads, it's less than a 10-minute hike to the Ditch Road crossing.

Po'omau Canyon Vista Trail

Easy effort
0.25 miles
Elevation gain 76 feet

Hwy.550, MM15.5—see Touring Mohihi Road. Drive (4x4 only) or hike 4.5 miles to Po'omau Canyon Vista trailhead. This short trail hikes through a tall old-growth

Sugi Pine grove for a couple hundred feet, then crosses a small foot bridge and Ditch Road. Old 'Ohi'a and koa trees take over as this wide, maintained trail drops in elevation reaching trail's end, offering beautiful elevated views of Po'omau and Waimea canyons. You'll hear the roar of Moeloa Falls but no view, you need to hike Ditch Trail, across the canyon, for that view.

View of Kauhoa Trail from Canyon Trail

Kohua Ridge Trail

High effort
2.6 miles
Elevation gain 761 feet

Hwy. 550, MM 15.5—see Touring Mohihi Road. Drive (4x4 only) or hike 5.2 miles to the Kohua Ridge trailhead.

The trail starts as a wide, double-track, then narrows to a single-track trail as you cross Ditch Road then down into the valley. Hop across the stream and hike up the steep hill with its deep erosion troughs. Once on top of Kohua Ridge the trail flattens out with only a few small up and downs to climb, then guides you out into the middle of a canyon trifecta.

You're on a ridge but it's lined on both sides with pristine jungle so you don't really feel the altitude until the halfway point. The views are spectacular of Poʻomau Canyon on the right, Koaie Canyon on the left, and Waimea Canyon at your 12 o'clock. Plenty pig on this trail, you'll see the diggings.

At the point, MM 2.6, there's an unexpected guardrail and a great place to hang out. Be safe. A 5-hour round-trip hike, elevation gain of 761 feet but remember the steep valley climb.

Mohihi Trail

High effort

4 miles

Elevation gain 679 feet

Hwy. 550, MM 15.5—see Touring Mohihi Road. Drive (4x4 only) or hike 6.2 miles to the end of the road, you'll find a covered picnic table and the trailhead.

The trail starts as a double-track, then crosses Ditch Road and narrows to a single-track trail behind the second picnic table. Cross the stream, which is the only water source until Koaie Campground at the end of the trail. Then climb uphill through a pine tree forest to MM 0.7, where the trail is maintained, widens, and plateaus until MM 2, a great day hike and one of the most pleasant jungle hikes I've ever walked. Just beyond MM 1 is the trail's highest elevation, there's an old bench to offer a rest and splendid panoramic views of Kokeʻe, from Alakaʻi Swamp to Koaie Canyon.

At MM 2, there's a small clearing with two steel poles cemented into the ground, the trail continues to your right. From here to Koaie Camp is a tight, single-track trail, the first half mile is a dried-fern hell with soft trail edges, wear leg gators...or else.

Then, the trail passes a cliff and switchbacks to your left up a short hill and into Mohihi's baby swamp and easier hiking. Moss, fern, mud, and 'Ohi'a trees delight and cool the senses on this flat terrain.

At MM 3.7 there's a steep descent into Koaie Camp and Mohihi stream, and it's *steep*. A technical and slippery section, use the roots, rocks, trees, and grass to hold onto, whatever it takes to conquer this bit of the trail, go slow and be safe. The solace here is that it's only a quarter-mile drop and camp is at the bottom of this hill. Six hours round trip, hiking time only, enjoy.

Water Tank Trail

Easy effort
1 mile
Elevation gain less than 100 feet
Hwy. 550, MM 15.9. Park at a small field at the trailhead or you can park at the museum and it's a short walk north to the trail.

A single-track trail that hikes through an old 'Ohi'a tree forest with plenty strawberry guava in the late fall months. The Water Tank Trail loops with the Pu'u Ka 'Ohelo Trail, or with the Berry Flats Trail further east, for a 3-mile loop, a 2.5-hour hike at a cruising pace.

Kaluapuhi Trail

Easy effort
1.2 miles
Elevation gain less than 100 feet
Hwy. 550, MM 17.3 for the trailhead, it also loops back

to the highway at MM 18.4. There's a fork at 0.3 miles, go left to stay on the trail, to the right is a hunting trail with tree-obstructed valley views.

This single-track trail opens into a wide, field-type hike for a non-claustrophobic trek. Beautiful, old-growth 'Ohi'a and guava trees line this flat, "all people welcome" trail. Please hike the trail back to your car, the highway has little, if no, soft shoulder to walk on, be safe. A 2-hour round-trip hike.

Waimea Canyon Base Hikes
Waimea Canyon Trail

High effort
10.5 miles
Elevation gain 735 feet

Hwy. 50, MM 21.5. In Waimea town, turn right at the fire station on Menehune Road. It's best to park at the foot bridge at MM 1.6, there's more space, then walk to the crossing a half mile upriver.

The trail itself is a *tote road* that connects with the Kukui Trail at MM 10 and the Koaie Canyon Trail at MM 10.5. You'll cross the snaking Waimea River 14 times to get to the tail end of Kukui Trail and Wiliwili Campground. Bring an old pair of sneakers or water shoes to cross the river and save your hiking boots for the drier parts.

The trail starts with five river crossings then, after changing back into your boots, climbs "rock hill" which turns into "sand hill", the highest elevation on the trail with grand views of the western canyon walls. Then you'll descend to the river for a nice, wooded forest and swimming hole.

At river crossing six, change back into your water

sneakers, you'll need them through river crossing 17 at the end of the trail, they're all fairly close together. This is where the the canyon narrows for steep, 360 degree views, it's beautiful and caressing.

Within a half-mile north of Wiliwili Camp is the second campsite, Kaluahaulu Camp. I prefer this camp, with mesmerizing valley views and pristine swimming holes. Koaie Canyon trailhead connects with Waimea Canyon Trail's end on the right at MM 10.5.

Pu'u Kaeha, Waimea Canyon Trail

Koaie Canyon Trail

High effort
3 miles
Elevation gain 965 feet

This single-track trail starts at the tail end of the Waimea Canyon Trail (a *tote road*). I grade this trail high effort because of the trailhead's location, the magnificent belly of the Waimea Canyon, it's a hike before the hike.

A tight trail that passes a few large *heiau* as the trail enters the forest groves in this picturesque valley. Hipalau Camp is about a mile in, but the prize is the last campsite on the trail at MM 3, Lonomea Campground.

Towards the end of the trail you'll cross the stream, making it 18 water crossings from Waimea town, and just past the emergency helicopter pad, you're there! Truly, this is one of the prettiest canyons on Earth, the superlative Koaie Canyon…enjoy.

NOTES

Gillin Beach from Mahaʻulepu Trail

<u>South Side Hike</u>
Mahaʻulepu Trail

Moderate effort
2.5 miles
Elevation gain 50 feet

Hwy. 50, MM 6.7. Turn on Hwy. 520 (the Tree Tunnel), go left at 2.7 miles onto Ala Kinoiki Road for another 2.8 miles to Poʻipu Road, go left for 0.5 miles, pass the Grand Hyatt and turn right at Ainako Road. Continue past the Poipu Bay Golf Course to the end of the road at Shipwrecks Beach.

Once at the sand, the trail starts to the left of the parking lot, then climbs the sandstone cliffs for amazing ocean views the entire trail, walking a portion along the Poipu Bay Golf Course, to Kawelikoa Point. You'll hike the Aweoweo Sand Dunes along the rugged lava rock and sandstone coastline (Kauaʻi's finest) onto Gillin Beach at MM 1.7, then around the bend onto Mahaʻulepu Beach.

At the far side of Mahaʻulepu Beach, the coastal trail continues on to another hidden beach at the end.

East Side Hikes

Sleeping Giant - Kuamoʻo Nounou Trail

Moderate effort
3.8 miles
Elevation gain 679 feet

Hwy. 56, MM 6. Turn on Hwy. 580-Kuamoʻo Road and drive 2.3 miles to the trailhead. Park roadside along the horse corral, step over the yellow gate and hike the wide, green belt, cross the foot bridge and you've already begun.

A thick forest of hau trees starts this single track trail. Hike uphill to a picnic table lookout with grand views of Wailua Valley, Makaleha Mountain, and Waiʻaleʻale Crater. Then it's a climb to the top of "Sleeping Giant" ridge.

The Nounou Trail hooks up with East and West Nounou Trails, go east and up the hill for panoramic views of Wailua Bay and the Wailua River, the widest river in Hawaiʻi. It's a soggy trail...bring mosquito spray. The moss-covered jungle alone is worth the hike, great photos! The strawberry guava peak in early September. The deep red ones are ripe and delicious. The west trail is a short hike that leads to a cliff lookout.

Kuilau Ridge Trail

Easy effort
2.1 miles
Elevation gain 558 feet

Hwy. 56, MM 6. Turn on Hwy. 580-Kuamoʻo Road and drive 6.7 miles to the trailhead and small parking lot.

Step over the yellow gate to start the wide, single-track trail with distant views of Polihale State Beach and the wet Mount Waiʻaleʻale (dumped a record 714 inches of rain in 1982). Kuilau Trail joins with Moalepe Trail for another 4.4 miles.

Small Falls, Loop Road

Keahua Arboretum - Loop Road

Moderate effort
4.8 miles
Elevation gain 876 feet

Hwy. 56, MM 6. Turn on Hwy. 580-Kuamoʻo Road and drive 6.8 miles to the end of the paved road. Park and hike, or 4x4, the 4.8-mile *tote road* to the end of the road, the start of Blue Hole Trail.

Check out the Rainbow Eucalyptus trees at the beginning of loop road, they're magically real! There are two stream crossings, one at the beginning of Loop Road and the second is 0.8 miles up the *tote road*, crossable by car when there's a slow water flow, then proceed carefully at your own risk. The Powerline trailhead is 0.2 miles on top of the first hill.

At the first fork at MM 2.6, go left, going to the right is just a waist-deep muddy hunting *tote road*. Warning: If you hear gunfire, hunting is permitted on weekends and holidays, please wear bright colors.

Back on Loop Road, drive to the fork at MM 3.8. To the right is the single-track Ka'apoko Trail, an 8-hour round-trip hike that takes you to the mile-long tunnel, bring a flash light and mosquito spray. It's always a muddy trail, after a while you'll stop walking the edges of the mud puddles and just plow straight through 'em.

The left fork at MM 3.8 will lead you to Blue Hole, 0.1 mile past the yellow gate are two cement posts which were the anchors for the huge gates from that famous dinosaur movie.

To find Blue Hole simply look up, it's not down at the water, the easterly trade winds hit the cliffs of Mount Wai'ale'ale and shoot straight up to bore a hole in the clouds, creating…a blue hole!

At the end of the road at MM 4.8, you'll get up close and personal with Mount Wai'ale'ale at your 12 o'clock and Waikoko Falls at your 10 o'clock, astounding at almost 1,000 feet.

Waiʻaleʻale Rains

Twin Falls / Blue Hole Pools

Hike or 4x4 Loop Road 4.8 miles to the end of the road. A muddy, 2-mile technical hike that starts at the right side of the river. Cross the river to your left at about MM 1, look carefully for the orange ribbon that the Park Rangers use as trail locators. After a few hundred feet, cross the river again to the right side banking and continue toward the end of the trail that leads you back to the water. Then rock hop the river a few hundred feet upstream to Twin Falls, a pair of beautiful, 25-foot waterfalls that join to create the Blue Hole pools.

Powerline Trail

High effort
13 miles
Elevation gain 1,841 feet

Hwy. 56, MM 6. Turn on Hwy. 580-Kuamoʻo Road and drive 6.8 miles to the end of the paved road at Keahua Arboretum and park. Cross the stream and hike up the *tote road* hill 0.2 miles to the trailhead.

A wide, double-track trail that hikes up and over the middle of Kauaʻi to the north. Impressive jungle and valley views for most of the way, then the trail plateaus off for the last couple miles. A long, hot hike during the summer months and muddy during the winter.

Moalepe Trail

Moderate effort
2.3 miles
Elevation gain less than 680 feet

Hwy. 56, MM 6. Turn on Hwy. 580-Kuamoʻo Road and drive to MM 2.7 and turn right at Kamalu Road, continue 1.6 miles to the end. Turn left and drive 1.5 miles to the trailhead and yellow gate on the corner of Olohena Road and Waipouli Road.

Park across the street and hike the wide, single-track trail with wonderful *mauka* views of Makaleha Mountain Range at your 2 o'clock. A green jungle hike that switchbacks into the valley, then joins with Kuilau Trail for a 4.4-mile hike to the Keahua Arboretum.

Ho'opi'i Falls Trail

Easy effort
1 mile
Elevation gain 180 feet

Hwy. 56, MM 9. Turn onto Kawaihau Road and drive 2.9 miles to Kapahi Road. Turn right, go 0.2 miles to the yellow-gated trailhead and park roadside.

A wide, single-track trail that hikes along Kapa'a Stream. Follow the stream to Baby Falls, a narrow 20-footer, then continue hiking downstream stream about a mile to the top of Ho'opi'i Falls, a 30-foot wonder.

To get to the base of the falls, look to the right up on the cliff, you'll see a trail that hikes about 100 yards, then descends steeply to the base of Ho'opi'i. Bring your bathing suit and mosquito spray. Green fields with mimosa, guava, and eucalyptus trees canopy this charming valley.

NOTES

Hanalei Bay

'Okolehao Trail

High effort
2.3 miles
Elevation gain 1,224 feet

Hwy. 560, MM 1.3. Turn left onto the paved road just past the Hanalei Bridge. Drive 0.6 miles to the trailhead and park across the street.

A steep, single-track trail that hikes up to Kaukaopua Lookout at 984 feet overlooking the majestic Hanalei Bay. High elevation makes for outstanding *makai* and *mauka* views. Green jungle, blue skies, and white clouds will enthrall.

The trail does continue another 2 miles up to Hihimanu Mountain but prepare for a steeper climb and watch for rain clouds, they move in quickly from the trade winds, and wet means slippery. Late summer sunsets over the bay are fantastic and strawberry guava peak in late summer.

Hanakapiʻai Falls Trail

High Effort
4 miles
Elevation gain 589 feet

The end of the Hwy. 560, MM 10-Keʻe Beach. For the first two miles you're hiking the famous Kalalau Trail. It's a wide, maintained, single-track trail that hikes over rock, mud, and dirt to a 558-foot peak elevation, with awe-inspiring Na Pali views along the way. One m.p.h. is an easy pace with photos, lunch, and a swim to plan your hike. The only water source is the Hanakapiʻai Stream, nothing is piped in so remember to treat or filter your stream water, Leptospirosis bacteria is present. This is important: being a hot and humid climate, you're going to drink a lot more water than expected, bring extra water, a treatment, or filter for this hike. Pack food, it will help keep your energy up. It is a demanding hike and well worth the effort.

Rock hop to the Hanakapiʻai Falls Trail that starts on the south side of Hanakapiʻai Stream at a 114-foot elevation. The trail splits at the outhouse, the right fork continues the Kalalau Trail, the left fork is the trailhead to the falls. You'll pass an emergency helicopter landing pad, then hike into tall bamboo fields. Listen for the music the bamboo make while dancing in the wind, it's pretty cool. About 1 mile in, you'll cross the stream twice, over a pennisula, within a couple hundred feet to the north bank. The trail narrows and gets a bit more technical from here to the falls, and it's always muddy. Park Rangers do a good job of trail marking by tying bright-colored ribbons to trees for trail locators, so follow *da kine*.

The trail hikes you to a 40-foot cliff, take a tricky left, then up and over it. Descend the cliff for the next steam crossing at "Beautiful Pool" a large, cool *puka* (perhaps the finest swimming hole on the island). Hike the south bank for a couple hundred feet, then cross the stream for the forth and final time to the north bank until the you reach the falls, and you're close. At this point you'll start to hear the thunder of the falls and get excited, but it's the baby 20-foot falls in the stream below. Hike up and over some large rocks, the most technical part of the trail and you'll find...your first view of Hanakapi'ai Falls, a 350-foot giant splashing into a fern-lined amphitheater. Start photographing from here to fit the whole falls into one shot, or break out the 10mm super wide lens at the falls' pool. Trail elevation at the pool is 703 feet. Safety note: more than just water comes over the falls, rocks, trees, even goats may also fall, beware.

Now for the hike out, it's all downhill from the falls to Hanakapi'ai Beach. Then it's back on the Kalalau Trail with some climbing back to Ke'e Beach.

Kalalau Spires by Sea

Kalalau Spires

Kalalau Trail

High effort
11 miles
Elevation gain 880 feet

The end of Hwy. 560, MM 10-Keʻe Beach. The grandpa of Kauaʻi's trails, stories will be told and legends will be made forever! The trailhead is at the end of the road on the north shore of Hwy. 560, Keʻe Beach. Parking's limited, so there's an overflow lot at MM 9.8 before the end of the road. Warning…don't park overnight, because when times are hard, people get desperate. Hitch hike, which is legal in Hawaiʻi, or bum a ride from Hanalei town and the last public bus stop if you're hiking the complete 11 miles, an overnighter at minimum—pack accordingly. Super men have hiked this challenging trail at a 2 m.p.h. pace, the rest of us hike the 1 m.p.h. easy pace with photos and rest stops. Kauaʻi's Na Pali Coast is one of the magnificent coastlines in the world. Four-thousand-foot cliffs of green jungle and waterfalls dropping straight down onto the Kalalau Trail then into the warm, clear-blue Pacific waters will mesmerize all who are lucky enough to gaze upon this majestic coastline.

There are six water sources that run year-round, Hanakapi'ai Stream 2 miles in, Waiahuakua Stream at MM 5, Hanakoa Stream at 6.3 miles, a baby falls and stream around MM 8, Kalalau Stream 10 miles in, and Aloha Falls at the south end of Kalalau Beach at 10.7 miles. The first of five emergency helicopter landing pads is at Windy Point, a half-mile in, the second is inland a couple hundred yards of Hanakapi'ai Beach at the 2 mile point, a third on the north side of Hanakoa Camp close to MM 6, the fourth is at MM 8, and the fifth is in between camp and the sand at Kalalau Beach. There are four toilets on the trail, the first and only flusher is at Ke'e Beach at the trailhead, also with your best chance of tissue being available. The remaining three are outhouses: at Hanakapi'ai Beach, on the north stream bank at Hanakoa Campground, and at the Kalalau Beach camp.

Elevation gain is deceptive on this enduring and endearing trail ranging from 22 feet at the trailhead at Ke'e Beach to the highest point, 902 feet, at the Hono O Na Pali gate about 3.5 miles in. You're constantly climbing or descending on the Kalalau, the coastal points being the highest elevation and the valleys, by the streams, the lowest spots.

The first half-mile of this wide, maintained single-track trail is demanding, simply because you're just starting the hike and haven't gotten your leg stamina yet. You'll climb over slippery rocks and roots up to Windy Point, a 480-foot elevation, and the first grand view of Na Pali. The trail flattens for a bit and you'll feel immediate relief, confidence will grow, and the hiking gets easier. Great tree canopy for shade covers the first mile to the

558-foot pinnacle, the highest elevation on the 2-mile stretch to Hanakapi'ai Beach, then it's time to unpack the hat for refuge from the sun. At any time of year, it gets hot quickly on this trail when there's no tree canopy or cloud cover. The trail then hikes you down into the first of many beautiful valleys and a small stream crossing, and up to the last point before the beach.

Hike down to Hanakapi'ai Beach at MM 2 which is a beautiful, round stone-lined beach in the winter and sandy in the summer months, ocean currents account for changes in beach condition. This is a good day hike. If you need a dip to cool down, do so in the river, do not swim at Hanakapi'ai Beach for safety's sake.

Rock hop the river to continue. The trail forks at the outhouse, to the right continues the Kalalau Trail and inward is the trailhead to the very impressive Hanakapi'ai Falls—see the Hanakapi'ai Falls Trail for details.

From Hanakapi'ai Beach south for the next 8 miles the trail narrows and is very technical. Take your time and always watch your footing. Start the climb up "Centipede Hill" an erosion-troughed switchback that hikes to amazing views of the south side of the beach and Hanakapi'ai Valley, at 2 miles deep she's a grand valley, and the first of four, each getting better as you hike south. Then it's off to the highest elevation point of the trail at 902 feet as you cross the Hono O Na Pali Nature Reserve's gate (a pig fence) close to 3.5 miles in. Rounding this point is were many feel the real fireworks of the Kalalau Trail begin with breathtaking Na Pali views, massive Waiahuakua Valley, and waterfalls greeting you and redefining nature as most know it. The trail switchbacks down and into an old-growth mango, mountain apple, and guava tree forest, for the start of fruit-bearing Na Pali jungle. Waiahuakua Valley is a welcomed rest as cold stream water and shade trees refresh at MM 5.

Hiking toward the north point of Hanakoa Valley is going to be a bit windy once on the coastline. Note: all coastal points are windy, some more than others and later in the day are always the strongest winds. Hike the trail to Hanakoa Campsite at MM 6.3, just past the halfway mark. There's the northside outhouse, and two sheltered picnic tables on each bank of the stream.

Hang out at the beautiful Hanakoa Falls less than half- mile in from the campsite. This waterfall is impressive, it's about a hundred feet taller (guesstimate) than Hanakapi'ai Falls, the pool is twice the size, and the valley walls are higher and narrower. It's fantastic and isolated. To get here, cross the stream and follow the trail east from the southern campsite, after about 300 feet cross the south fork of the stream, you'll see a 7-foot waterfall a little further east of the trail, continue on. Look for bright-colored ribbons that mark the trail. Hike up through jungle forest, old *heiau* and *kauhale*, with wild blueberries and guava lining the cliff trail for about a half-mile. You'll hear the falls before you see it, turn the corner to the right and you're there.

For those of you not hiking straight through to Kalalau Beach, you can camp here at Hanakoa overnight to rejuvenate yourself, it's an exhausting hike and your muscles need time to recover. I've seen world-class athletes cry after hiking the famed Kalalau Trail and the only cure for fatigue is rest. **From this point south you'll need a camping permit, found online at www. hawaiistateparks.org.**

Continuing on to Kalalau Beach from this point

it seems like a different trail, it's drier, the thick jungle goes away, and it seems the winds are stronger. This is a good place to unpack your hat with a chin strap and sunscreen. The soil is dry so footing is loose and slippery here, it seems like desert for the next mile. The trail has been improved over the years but still demands full attention, as does the entire trail. At MM 7 is the infamous "Crawler's Ledge", when crossing the Ledge it's best to hold your walking sticks in your right hand and use you left arm to brace yourself against the cliff wall for stability. You can do it, thousands of hikers a year do it! It's the same narrow trail you've been hiking for 7 miles there's just no vegetation hiding the slopes.

MM 8 is where the jungle starts to thicken again and there's a cool steam at this small valley. The third helicopter landing pad is here. Rounding the next couple of points will put you in the middle of yucca tree heaven and great coastal views. Look for squirrel rock and huge sea caves. From mile 8.75 to 9.5 the trail levels out more than usual, and the anticipation grows as the mountains seem to swell and the ocean waters get a clearer, brilliant blue.

Pass a few more small valleys and stand on "Red Hill", the gateway to Kalalau Valley, overlooking one of *Pele*'s masterpieces. At more than 3 miles deep, 2 miles wide, and walls higher than 4,000 feet, Kalalau Valley is monumental. Red cliffs and green-jungle floor compliment each other vividly. Add long views of Na Pali from Kalalau Beach to Miloli'i Beach and you've won the game of life. And as a bonus, the 2,000-foot Kalalau Spires stand tall on the south valley walls. Hiking down red hill into the Kalalau Valley jungle is amazingly easy, kind of magical. The trail continues at the plateau north of the jungle canopy, about a quarter-mile in you'll reach the Kalalau Stream and start to see rouge campers. Cross the stream to plentiful campsites and the beach. Set up camp and enjoy, this is victory. Peace, happiness, and love will show itself at Kalalau like no other place on Earth.

South of Kalalau Beach are Honopu, Miloli'i and Nu'alolo beaches, open May 15 through Labor Day. There are no hiking trails to these beaches but beach landings by kayak are permitted. The Na Pali Coast State Wilderness Park is the largest state park in Hawai'i at 6,175 acres.

Kalalau Valley Trail
Up the Kalalau Valley Trail 2.7 miles is Waimakemake Falls, a triple lava tube waterfall with the lower 100-foot falls visible at the trail's end at the pool.

The trailhead is on the south side of Kalalau Stream, the trail is wide and heavily traveled for the first 1.9 miles passing *kauhale* and fruit trees on the way. At the end of the main trail, at 1.9 miles, starts the very narrow and technical portion that leads you to the falls for another 0.8 miles. As the trail changes it's personality changes also, from a wide, jungle forest hike to a stream-side, thick jungle hike with moss-covered rocks and stumps, it's beautiful.

About a third of a mile in, you hike up the side of a 50-foot cascade, not really a falls, but a few hundred yards later you'll hike up a true 50-foot falls and it's only 15 minutes to Waimakemake Falls from here. There are six stream crossings on the hike to the falls, with an elevation of about 1,200 feet.

Gentle Ben

Open Ceiling Cave by Boat

THE ISLAND OF
KAUA'I

533 sq. miles
90 miles of coastline
33 miles E to W
25 miles N to S

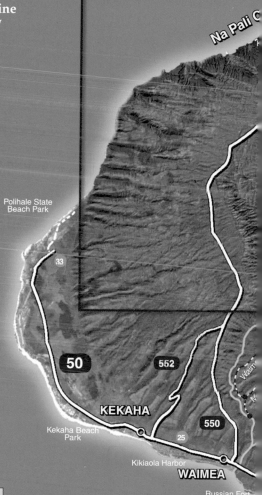

See Waimea Canyon State Park and
Koke'e State Park Detailed Map

Na Pali C

Polihale State
Beach Park

33

50

552

550

KEKAHA

Kekaha Beach
Park

25

Kikiaola Harbor

WAIMEA

Russian Fort

omoneyfunguidebooks.com

Satelite image courtesy of NASA

NOTES

Beach Combing / Road Tripping

<u>South of Lihuʻe</u>
Kalapaki Beach

Hwy. 51-Kapule Highway to Rice Street and turn left, or Hwy. 58-Nawiliwili Road will bring you to Nawiliwili Bay and Kalapaki Beach.

A couple miles east of Lihuʻe town, park and walk the foot bridge behind Anchor Cove Shopping Center. A sand beach with an easy, slow-breaking wave great for the beginner surfers, good snorkeling on the east side of the bay. It's in front of a big resort for a refreshing drink when needed, and there are plenty of rental shops for surfboards and everything else.

Menehune Fishpond

Menehune Fishpond

From Rice Street, continue onto Hwy. 58-Nawiliwili Harbor. Turn left on Wilcox Road and drive 0.2 miles, turn right on Niumalu Road, pass the cruise ship Pier 2 and drive 0.5 miles, turn right onto Hulemalu Road and drive to the lookout at 0.5 miles.

Many stories have been written about the fishpond and each and every one is different. So simply enjoy the moment, the Menehune Fishpond and Hoary Head Mountain Range are beautiful.

Tree Tunnel

Hwy. 50, MM 6.7. Turn on Hwy. 520-Maluhia Road and you're at Kaua'i's famous Tree Tunnel.

A tunnel of eucalyptus trees planted for shade over a hundred years ago for visitors to the south shore and the cane workers of Koloa. On the north end of the tunnel, you'll see philodendron growing up the trees. Your common house plant…on steroids!

Koloa Town

Hwy. 50, MM 6.7. Turn on Hwy. 520-Maluhia Road and drive 3.1 miles into Koloa Town.

The first successful sugar cane plantation in the state of Hawai'i was founded here by Ladd & Co. in 1835. Old Koloa Town has a small museum, and across the street in the park is an old chimney from the first cane mill in the islands, built in 1841, and is now a U.S. National Monument. Also check out the old monkeypod trees of Koloa…your grandparents knew these trees.

Keonıloa Bay - Shipwrecks Beach

Shipwrecks Beach

Hwy. 50, MM 6.7. Turn on Hwy. 520-Maluhia Road and drive 2.7 miles to Ala Kinoiki Road, turn left and drive 2.8 miles to Po'ipu Road. Turn left on Po'ipu Road and go 0.5 miles, passing the Grand Hyatt, to Ainako Road and turn right for 0.2 miles, continue past the Poipu Bay Golf Course to the small parking lot at the end of the road.

Good shore break for advanced body boarding and surfing. The trailhead to the Maha'ulepu Trail starts to the left and continues for 2.5 miles. Up on Pa'a Dunes, the sandstone cliffs, is a great spot for colorful sunsets.

Green Honu

Po'ipu Beach Park

Hwy. 50, MM 6.7. Turn on Hwy. 520-Maluhia Road and drive 3.1 miles to Koloa Town. Turn right onto Koloa Road and take the first left onto Po'ipu Road. Drive 1.4 miles to the traffic circle, take the third exit and continue on Po'ipu Road for 0.9 miles to Mano O Kalanipo Park. Turn right onto Ho'owili Road for one block and park.

An excellent snorkeling beach with Nukumoi Island about 40 walkable feet off the beach. Brennecke's Beach, to the east, is a nice shore break with sand base for boogie boarders and body surfers. Keep a look out for *honu*, they're around. The park is complete with showers, flush toilets, pavilions with BBQ pits, a *keiki* jungle gym, and lifeguard tower.

Koloa Landing

Hwy. 50, MM 6.7. Turn on Hwy. 520-Maluhia Road and drive 3.1 miles to Koloa Town. Take a right on Koloa Road, then the first left on Po'ipu Road, follow 1.4 miles to the traffic circle and take the second exit on Lawa'i Road. Take your first left and cross the bridge to the first parking shoulder 0.1 miles on the right. Walk down the slope, you're there.

Great scuba diving and snorkeling, most of the south shore dive companies dive here. Originally, Koloa Landing was the harbor for the cane ships, before Nawiliwili Harbor was built. Look for old train tracks, *honu*, and Dragon Moray Eels.

Lawa'i Road and Ho'ai Beach

Hwy. 50, MM 6.7. Turn on Hwy. 520-Maluhia Road and drive 0.1 miles to Koloa Road, turn right on Koloa Road, then left onto Po'ipu Road. Drive 1.4 miles to the traffic circle and take the second exit on Lawa'i Road.

At 0.4 miles is Kuhio Park. As grandson to King Kaumuali'i, Kaua'i's last king, Prince Kuhio served in the House of Representatives in Washington D.C. for 20 years in the early 20th century and implemented the Hawaiian Homes Commission Act.

Ho'ai Beach is 0.5 miles down Lawa'i Road, a prime snorkeling spot that has showers and flush toilets. Baby Beach is at 0.7 miles, look for the waist-high lava rock wall. This is where toddlers hang while Mom and Dad take turns surfing Acid Drop, Centers, and P.K.'s.

At 1.3 miles is Kukui'ula Boat Harbor, another good snorkel spot. The National Tropical Botanical Garden's Allerton Garden and McBryde Garden, are at 1.7 miles. Be prepared to take some time, you'll need a week to absorb all the splendor of the gardens. To get a taste, at the visitor's center outside of the valley, there are 10 acres of plantings with lotus ponds to roam for free, ahh...No Money Fun!

Spouting Horn

Follow the directions above to Lawaʻi Road and Hoʻai Beach. From the Poʻipu traffic circle, drive 1.8 miles on Lawaʻi Road to Spouting Horn. During summer south swells the spout really blows big, but all year long it goes good at high tides. Listen and you'll hear the cries and hissing of the trapped *moʻo* trying to get free. A good place for winter sunsets.

Kauai Coffee Company

Hwy. 50, MM 12.4. Turn on Hwy. 540 and drive 2.5 miles to the Kauai Coffee Company Visitor Center, gift shop, and museum.

There are some "No Money Fun" *ono* coffee samples on the *lanai*, also a free self-guided walking tour. This is the largest coffee plantation in America with over four million trees.

Hanapepe Valley Lookout

Hwy. 50, MM 14.1. Roadside parking. While driving towards the Hanapepe Valley Lookout, the view is obscured by thick jungle then… bam! All of Kauaʻi opens up. High, red dirt cliffs and deep views of Hanapepe Valley appear. The famous Jurassic Falls is a few miles into this valley. Remember, this lookout is only an appetizer of what the Waimea Canyon offers.

Port Allen and Glass Beach

Hwy. 50, MM 16. Turn left onto Waialo Road and the port is a stone's throw to the ocean.

Lots of boat charters sail from here, think Na Pali cruises and deep sea fishing. Port Allen is Kauaʻi's first commercial seaport, an exciting place to be a hundred years ago with beer, brothels, and bar fights.

Glass Beach, *makai* side of the electric company smoke stacks, is an old dump site, hence the glass. Bring a shovel to dig with, the surface glass has been picked clean. There's a nice coastal hike east of the port with lava arches.

Hanapepe Town

Hwy. 50, MM 16.3. Turn right onto Hanapepe Road and follow it through this quaint, old town. Being one of Kaua'i's art districts, Friday nights are a good stroll with an Art Walk from 6 p.m. to 9 p.m., you know, complimentary wine and *pupus*.

Salt Pond Beach Park

Salt Pond Beach Park

Hwy. 50, MM 17.1. Turn left on Hwy. 543-Lele Road, drive past the veteran cemetery and go right on Lolokai Road to Salt Pond.

A county beach park with a lifeguard tower, showers, flush toilets, and permit-only camping. Great tide pool swimming and snorkeling, catch the sun setting from here close to Ni'ihau for most of the year. Also, check out the locals farming salt, it's a cool time-warp thing.

Russian Fort State Park

Hwy. 50, MM 22.7. *Makai* side just before the Waimea River. A historical state park named Fort Elizabeth after the Empress of Russia at the time. Built in 1817 with permission from the last king of Kaua'i, King Kaumuali'i. 17.3 acres.

Waimea Town

Hwy. 50, MM 23. While crossing the Waimea River bridge look left out into the bay, this is where Captain Cook anchored his ship for the first time in Hawai'i waters in 1778. There's a statue of him at the park in this small, 1940s-type town. An old Mission House and movie theater capture Waimea's charm. The black sand beach at MM 21.6 has one of only three fishing piers on Kaua'i. Say hello to my fishing lady friends, who age from 10 to 110, and taught me how to fish the Hawaiian shoreline.

A must do: West Kaua'i Technology and Visitor Center is a museum-type visitor center loaded with wonderful cultural artifacts and story. Ever see a 21'1" solid koa wood outrigger canoe from 1880? Check out old photos and the gift shop, it's Hawaiian heritage at it's finest. There's free wifi and use of computers. To support the Visitor's Center visit the gift shop with Ni'ihau shell jewelry, koa wood carvings, and other locally made products. Donations are appreciated, it helps support the *hui*.

Free guided walking tour of Waimea town, lei

making, and hula lessons are offered throughout the week. Call (808) 338-1332 for reservations and hours. 9565 Kaumualii Highway, Waimea.

ʻŌhiʻa Tree and More, Puʻu O Kīla

Waimea Canyon and Kokeʻe State Parks

Hwy. 50, MM 23.3. Turn onto Hwy. 550—see Touring Hwy. 550 *p.7*. This is a scenic road with lookouts along the first 6 miles. Thick, koa tree jungle lines the road until you reach MM 8.7, Kukui Trail, for your first true view of Waimea Canyon.

Kokeʻe State Park is adjacent to Waimea Canyon State Park and starts at MM 14.1, then continues to the end of the road, Puʻu O Kila Lookout...the prettiest spot on Earth.

For a detailed guide of these parks and their trails refer to Hiking *Makai* and *Mauka* sides of Waimea Canyon and Kokeʻe. For the ultimate sunset view close to Niʻihau, drive 6.2 miles up Hwy. 552, or down 1.2 miles from the fork at Hwy. 550, to a small roadside parking shoulder and enjoy.

Kikiaola Small Boat Harbor

Hwy. 50, MM 24.8. A small, jettied boat harbor with ramp. Some boat tours and charters launch here. Good hammerhead shark fishing off the jetties.

Kekaha Beach Park

Hwy. 50, MM 25.3. Where the black sand ends and the light yellow sand begins is Kekaha Beach Park. Here offers your first views of "the Forbidden Island" of Ni'ihau and the atoll of Lehua 17 miles offshore. The stretch of sand from Kekaha to Polihale is 17 miles, the longest sand beach in the state of Hawai'i. Beach combing anyone? Lifeguard tower and pavilions are on site.

Bottlenose Dolphins

Polihale State Beach

Hwy. 50, MM 33. Turn left on the dirt *tote road* at the road sign and drive 5.2 miles to the end of the road, or turn off at any road starting from the big monkeypod tree and these will bring you to any part of Polihale State Beach.

The north end of the beach is the start of the

sensational Na Pali Coast and Polihale Valley. At the south end of the beach is Queen's Pond, then Barking Sands Beach.

Polihale is a wonderful tent campsite by permit only with flush toilets, showers, and plenty of space for everyone. A portion of the south end of Polihale is closed to civilians, it's a Navy thing. Good shore break waves, but beware of the strong ocean currents. Beach combing for sunrise shells is never a morning wasted. Summer sand does get hot on the feet, bring your *slippers*. Polihale State Beach Park is 137.7 acres.

North of Lihuʻe
ʻAhukini Landing

Hwy. 570-ʻAhukini Road. Drive towards the Lihuʻe Airport, turn left at the first fork and follow ʻAhukini Road past the heliport to the end of the road.

From here is a great view of Hanamaʻulu Bay, choppy east coast waters, and the shoreline up to Kapaʻa. The pier is old and torn up, then patched, from hurricanes, yet fun to fish. The original pier launched boats filled with beef to feed the 1849 gold rush folks in California, being cheaper than sailing around South America from the east coast of the U.S. at the time (no Panama Canal).

Wailua Falls

Hwy. 56, MM 1.1. Turn on Hwy. 583-Maʻalo Road and drive 3.8 miles to the end of the road. Parking is tight, but the view of Wailua Falls, a 120-foot beauty, is spectacular and it's the closest to a major falls you can drive to. There's a wall to photograph from and a good chance you'll see the white-tailed tropicbirds feeding and flying.

Wailua Falls

Nukoli‘i Beach

Hwy. 56, MM 3.7. Turn on the road just south of the Wailua Municipal Golf Course (the best deal on 18 holes of golf in the U.S.). The road immediately turns into a dirt road, drive 0.5 miles until you reach this long sand beach.

Solid coral reef up to the sand line makes for good offshore fishing. This beach offers a good look at the wild, choppy east side surf with strong onshore trade winds… kiting anyone? Kaua‘i's beaches are unique, visit them all. Beach combing north all the way to Wailua Bay is possible from Nukoli‘i Beach.

Lydgate State Beach Park

Hwy. 56, MM 5.1. Turn on Leho Drive for 0.4 miles, then turn right on Nalu Road for 0.2 miles and you're there.

There's plenty of parking and a jungle gym that any 8-year-old at heart would go crazy for, it's grand! On the *makai* side, there's a large man-made tide pool for the safest east coast swimming on Kaua‘i. Lifeguard tower included.

At the north end of the parking lot there's the Hauola "City of Refuge" *Heiau*. If you upset the *ali'i*, you'd live there until forgiven...or else. The Hikina a ka la *Heiau* and the Wailua River mouth (the widest river in the state of Hawai'i) are also here. On rocks at the river mouth are petroglyphs uncovered by the seasonal tides in the summer.

Wailua Bay

Hwy. 56, MM 6.2. This is the bay and land of the *ali'i*, Kaua'i's royal *'ohana*. Death was the penalty for uninvited common folk found on this property. Hawaiians were always serious about protocol. After touring Hwy. 580-Kuamo'o Road, you'll know why the kings chose this wedge of land, from Mount Wai'ale'ale to Wailua Bay, to live.

Big Water Opaeka'a Falls

Kuamo'o Road

Hwy. 56, MM 6. Turn on Hwy. 580-Kuamo'o Road, a favorite east side drive. At 0.2 miles is the Holoholoku

TOURING KUAMO'O RD.

MM 0 Coco Palms Hotel
MM 0.1 Wailua River State Park
MM 0.2 Holoholoku Heiau
MM 1.4 Lookout Wailua River and Bay
MM 1.5 Opeaka'a Falls
MM 2.3 Sleeping Giant - Kuamo'o Nounou Trail *p.39*
MM 4.3 Hindu Temple
MM 4.7 Rainbow Eucalyptus Trees
MM 4.8 Back lot of the temple
MM 4.9 Kaua'i Research Center
MM 6.7 Kuilau Trail *p.40*
MM 6.8 Keahua Arboretum - Loop Road *p.41*

Heiau, the Royal Birth Stone, and up the stairs in the back is an old Japanese cemetery. Drive 1.4 miles to the Wailua Bay Lookout and the Poli'ahu *Heiau*.

At 1.5 miles on the right is the beautiful, 197-foot Opaeka'a Waterfall and across the street is a great view of the snaking Wailua River all the way to Mount Ha'upu. The Nounou hiking trail (the "Sleeping Giant") is at MM 2.3.

Continuing up Kuamo'o to the Wailua Rise, turn left at MM 4.3 onto Kaholalele Road and go 0.2 miles to the Hindu Temple and her spectacular Wailua River rim acreage. At MM 6.7 is the trailhead for the Kuilau Trail, and at 6.8 miles is the Keahua Arboretum and the end of the paved road, check out the Rainbow Eucalyptus Trees. This is also the start of Loop Road, refer to the Keahua Arboretum - Loop Road hike to guide you.

Old Kapa'a Town

Hwy. 56, MM 8.2. This is the nightlife on this sleepy little island. There's an old, main street-type town with shops and restaurants. Along the coral-shelved beaches there's a walking and biking path, called Ke Ala Hele Makalae, that follows the coastline from Kapa'a town to Donkey Beach for 4.3 miles.

Whale Tail

Kealia Beach

Hwy. 56, MM 10.2. Plenty of parking, a wonderful east side bay that has onshore trade winds and choppy waters, but the locals still surf 'em. Any day surfing is better than no day surfing. A long, sand beach with a jetty on the north end and the Kapa'a Stream emptying into the bay on the south side. Restrooms, showers, pavilions, lifeguards, and the walking and biking coastal path are accessible from here.

Donkey - Kumukumu Beach

Hwy. 56, MM 11.5. There's a 20 car parking lot with restrooms at the path's beginning, walk down to the coastal path, maybe 0.2 miles, then just to the right is access to the beach. A favorite, it's a secluded, fairly long sand beach that has shade trees, plenty of elbow room, and sometimes great-shaped waves.

Anahola Bay

Hwy. 56, MM 13.5. Turn right onto Anahola Road and drive 0.7 miles to the large, sandy beach on this big bay.

"Unreals" is the first section you park at, then you have the river mouth, and Anahola Beach Lots to the north. There's a coastal lava rock hike from Unreals to the point, then you can walk south for miles.

Kong Mountain

Hwy. 56, MM 14.8. Turnout, roadside parking northbound, this is your best viewing location of Kong Mountain. Look *mauka* side to the highest peak in the middle, that's the top of his cranium with Kong's facial profile, belly, and sloping shoulders on the left. Now look to the left of Kong, that's *Honu* Rock with the head of the turtle facing Kong. Okay, now look to the right of Kong, that's Hippo Mountain with the nose facing Kong, the bulging eyes, tiny hippo ears, and large body…cool ya!

Moloaʻa Bay

Hwy. 56, MM 16.6. Turn right at the fruit stand- Koʻolau Road and drive through the valley, Kaʻapuna *Hui* Lands, 1.1 miles to Moloaʻa Road, turn right and drive 0.8 miles to the end of the road. Park roadside, walk a couple of minutes to the beach, and I know you'll appreciate this sequestered jewel of a bay.

Larson's Beach

Hwy. 56, MM 19.9. Turn right onto Koʻolau Road and drive 1.1 miles to an unmarked dirt road, go left for 1 mile and park at the end.

A short, 10-minute hike gets you to this long, sand beach with lava rock at both ends to isolate this beautiful, untamed ocean and beach. Be careful of the strong ocean currents on the north side…it seems to be washing everybody's bathing suits off, we call them "the all over *hui*" because they tan all over.

Rock Quarry - Kahili Beach
Hwy. 56, MM 21.6. Turn right onto Wailapa Road, drive 0.4 miles and turn left on the dirt road, go 0.5 miles to the end of the road and park. A charming bay with sand beach, Makolea Point, and Kilauea Stream to the north. Please respect the island and pack out what you pack in, *mahalo*.

Secrets - Kauapea Beach
Hwy. 56, MM 23.9. Turn right onto the first Kalihiwai Road, drive 0.2 miles and turn onto the dirt road, then go 0.5 miles to the end and park. Hike 15 minutes down the path and you're there.

Great sand, surf, and sea-level views of Kilauea Lighthouse and Moku'aeae Island. Beware: the strong ocean currents on the south side almost always wash the suits off sunbathers here, no worries though, plenty banana leaf to cover your *u'i*, enjoy.

Kalihiwai Bay
Hwy. 56, MM 23.9. Turn right onto the first Kalihiwai Road. Look for the *makai* side waterfall at the far end of the first guardrail at 0.4 miles before you drive down to the beach, then continue 0.8 miles for a great birds-eye-view of Anini Beach (single car parking only, be snappy) and onto the end of the road another 1.1 miles and park. A large and gorgeous bay with high cliffs, sand beach, pristine warm waters, shade pines, and Kalihiwai River mouth. An extraordinary place and a great way to spend the day.

Back out on Hwy. 56 at MM 24.9 there's a guardrail

with a cement wall in the middle, look *mauka* side for a 40-foot waterfall, it's close, so close that if your windows are rolled down you could get wet.

Anini Beach Park

Hwy. 56, MM 25. Turn right onto the second Kalihiwai Road and drive 0.2 miles, turn left on Anini Road and it's 1.4 miles to the beach park with tent camping and boat ramp. Excellent coastal views, superb snorkeling for *keiki* on this shallow coral reef bay, and after a storm it's Kaua'i's best shell hunting beach.

Continuing on Hwy. 56 at MM 26.6, just past the Princeville Golf Course entrance, is a favorite north shore appetizer, pull off the road and look ahead in the distance...you'll see the majestic mountains of Hanalei!

Hideaway's - Kenomene Beach

Hwy. 56, MM 27.9. Turn right into the Princeville community on Ka Haku Road, drive 2.1 miles to a small beach access parking lot on the right and the path is in between the fences. The climb down to the beach is steep but worth it. This narrow, sand beach is special, secluded, and has quadruple overhead surf during big winter swells, what else could you ask for? Take your snorkel gear in case it's a calm, flat day on the water.

Taro Fields Lookout

Hwy. 560, MM 0.2. A roadside lookout with a birds-eye-view of the taro fields of Hanalei framed by the Namolokama Mountains, it's a sight to see!

Hanalei Bay Lookout

Hwy. 560, MM 0.7. A quick, roadside turnout with big

Hanalei Bay views and sunsets…a must stop.

Hanalei Sunset

Hanalei Town and Bay

Hwy. 560, MM 2.7. This is a wonderful, fairy-tale type town. Any right turn will get you to the bay. The first street is Aku Road, drive to Weke Road, turn right to get to the pier and Black Pot Beach or turn left for Pine Trees (Waioli Beach). Pine Trees hosts an occasional surf contest. Hanalei is the hometown of world surfing champions past and future. Here you'll get fantastic summer sunsets and huge winter surf.

At MM 2.9 is a great taro field and mountain photo op, and at MM 3.1 the "green church" of Hanalei. Continuing past the bridge is Middle's (Waipa) Beach, and at MM 4.5 is Waikoko Beach with clean waves and tight roadside parking.

Kahalahala Beach and Lumahai Beach

Hwy. 560, MM 4.8. Roadside parking. The celebrated movie beach and a north shore favorite is Kahalahala

Beach, a 2-minute walk down the dirt path gets you there. It's a sandy cove with lava rock islands within throwing distance from the beach that makes for great summertime swimming and snorkeling. You will experience love here, any and all love.

For safety's sake, always wear fins while swimming in any ocean, they work. Be careful in the strong winter waters, the beach drops steeply into the ocean, making it challenging or impossible to climb out and back onto the sand. During winter months, please beware of ocean conditions and watch for big surf.

Lumahai Beach, a long, wide sand beach, is around the point to the west at MM 5.8, roadside parking before the bridge. Here, the Lumahai River mouth empties into the ocean with good fishing and beach combing.

Kahalahala Beach

Wainiha Bay

Hwy. 560, MM 7.1. A narrow sandbar of a beach that's great for shell hunting. Plenty of choppy ocean water and the Wainiha River are here to delight.

Recorded as home to the oldest Hawaiian settlement in the islands, since around 200 A.D. In the early 19th century, the U.S. Census Bureau recorded 65 Menehune Nationalists living in Wainiha. It's a wondrous place with her valley to equal none other. You can get a birds-eye-view of Wainiha from the Kilohana Lookout at the end of the Alakai'i Swamp Trail in Koke'e.

Tunnels

Hwy. 560, MM 8.7. It's best to park at Ha'ena State Beach, walk to the water, turn right and go 0.2 miles to the point, you're there.

Great coral reef for snorkeling during summer months, the water gets large and wild in the winter. The tunnels are burrowed through the coral reef and leads to a drop off, then to an outer reef, it's an exciting dive or snorkel.

Ha'ena Beach Park

Hwy. 560, MM 8.8. A park whose beach stretches 2 miles from Ha'ena to Ke'e Beach, at the end of Hwy. 560. Beautiful, light sand beaches with high cliffs dropping straight down next to Hwy. 560. Camping by permit. Flush toilets, showers, lifeguard tower, and sometimes vendors all add to your comfort. Beach combing all the way to Ke'e Beach is an amazing walk. A 65.7 acre park.

Manininiholo Dry Cave

Hwy. 560, MM 8.8. Across from Ha'ena Beach, you can walk into the cave for about 100 yards without a flashlight. The cave is large and cool (both meanings), then gets dark and narrow for about...I don't know, I got scared and ran out.

Waikanaloa and Waikapalae Wet Caves

Hwy. 560, MM 9.8. Roadside, with limited short-term parking. Small ponds with an unusual blue water. The ceiling is what impresses most, primitive life, Mother Nature's Sistine Chapel. Is this how we all began?

Na Pali Backwash

Ke'e Beach

Hwy. 560, MM 10. The end of the road is Ke'e Beach and the start of Kalalau Trail and the Na Pali Coast State Wilderness Park, the largest state park in Hawai'i. The beach is a favorite. You'll be floating in the warm ocean tide pools of Ke'e, look up and there'll be the 2,000-foot cliffs of Na Pali, recognizing Bali Hai as you lay back with amazement and feel the caress of Kaua'i's grace hold you. Exposed root masses of Ironwood Pines line the beach, around the point to your left are sea-level views of Na Pali. Flush toilets, showers, and lifeguard tower are on site.

Little Money Lots of Fun
Kaua'i Museum

Hwy. 50 to 4428 Rice Street in Lihu'e. Located on the last block of Rice Street before intersecting with Hwy. 50. A must- see. Kauaian and Ni'ihau treasures of past and present fill two buildings with historical and priceless artifacts. Get up close and personal with a solid koa wood outrigger canoe, a feathered lei that was presented to WH Sloggett by King Kamehameha IV, Ni'ihau Shell lei, ancient stone tools, a model of Captain Cook's ship the "Resolution", wonderful original paintings and antique furniture. Accurate, cultural facts are plentiful from the island's first settlers to present-day Kaua'i and Ni'ihau dwellers.

Exhibits are changing every couple months to keep things hopping. General admission is $10 and as low as free for keiki 5 years old and under. And how's this for generosity? Your ticket is good for one week from the date of purchase. Visit www.kauaimuseum.org or call (808) 245-6931.

Wailua Municipal Golf Course

Hwy. 56, MM 4.3. The best golf deal in America, 18 holes on the coastline for dirt cheap, cash-only green fees. A bucket of balls for around $4 and beers for a couple of bucks, duff away! 3-5350 Kuhio Highway, Lihue. Call (808) 241-6666.

Limahuli Garden

Hwy. 560, MM 9.5. Set in a breathtaking, steep-walled valley with Bali Hai peak a stone's throw away. Voted "the Best Natural Botanical Garden in the U.S." by the American Horticultural Society and winner of the Koa

Award, this garden is the preeminent Hawaiian garden. This magnificent valley is owned by the non-profit National Tropical Botanical Garden, along with Allerton Garden and McBryde Garden on the south shore.

There's an inexpensive self-guided walking tour available all day from 9:30 a.m. to 4:00 p.m., guided tours are sometimes offered. A must-see! 5-8291 Kuhio Highway, Hanalei. Visit www.limahuli.ntbg.org or call (808) 826-1053 for pricing and tour information.

Kilauea Lighthouse

Kilauea Lighthouse and National Wildlife Refuge
Hwy. 56, MM 23.3. Turn right on Kolo Road for 0.2 miles, then left on Kilauea Road and drive 1.6 miles to the end of the road lookout. Check out the cliffs, seabirds, and the prettiest turquoise-colored bay in the world, high noon is the best time to view the bay.

Now drive down to the 52-foot Kilauea Lighthouse built in 1913, and watch for the great frigatebirds, with their 7.6-foot wingspan, Laysan albatross, Red-footed boobies, Red-tailed tropicbirds, and state bird, the *nene*. In winter waters, Humpback whales are plentiful, year-round there are spinner dolphins, *honu*, and helpful volunteers ready to be enjoyed. All Federal Lands Recreation Passes are honored here. Call (808) 828-1413 for pricing and information about ranger-led interpretive programs.

Kaua'i Mini Golf

Hwy. 56, MM 23.5. A challenging, 18-hole miniature golf course with water traps, bridges, and tunnels set in a beautiful tropical garden, have you ever seen black taro before? Also a concession stand serving hamburgers, pizza, gelato, and other treats is ready to delight.

There's finally something to do (besides drink) at night on Kaua'i, the last tee off is 8 p.m. Located in Kilauea off Hwy. 56, 0.3 miles west of the gas station. 5-2723 Kuhio Highway, Kilauea. Visit www.kauaiminigolf. com or call (808) 828-2118 for pricing.

Glossary

MM .... mile marker
aloha .... all that's good, greetings
mahalo .... thank you
tote road .... 4x4 drivable dirt road
mauka .... mountain
makai .... ocean
heiau .... place of worship
ali'i ....chief, royalty
small kine .... no worries
da kine .... you know, that thing
'ohana .... family
keiki .... children
ono .... delicious
plenty .... choke
choke .... plenty
slippers .... flip-flops
lanai .... porch
honu .... sea turtle
moa .... chicken
hui .... gang
mo'o.. lizard
talk story .... chat
no grumble ....'cause it's against the law on Kaua'i
braughda .... friend
u'i .... beautiful
pupus .... appetizers
nene......................................Hawaiian goose
puka... hole
Pele...................................... Hawaiian Volcano Goddess
kauhale.....................................village, homes